Gallery Books
Editor: Peter Fallon

THE CLARE ISLAND SURVEY

Seán Lysaght

THE
CLARE ISLAND
SURVEY

Gallery Books

The Clare Island Survey
is first published
simultaneously in paperback
and in a clothbound edition
in October 1991.

The Gallery Press
Loughcrew
Oldcastle
County Meath
Ireland

ISBN 1 85235 063 6 (*paperback*)
    1 85235 064 4 (*clothbound*)

The Gallery Press receives financial assistance from An Chomhairle
Ealaíon / The Arts Council, Ireland.

Contents

for my father

The Clare Island Survey

1

I have the sketch of Clare Island,
in your hand. You drew the great brow
in silhouette from the mainland,
and scribbled gulls over a blue sound,
then etched a furze bush
with pencilled spikes in the foreground
and, in between, some trees, a slate roof
and a red gable huddling together.
No sooner had I left two years ago
than you made our trip, on your own, to Mayo.

2

It lures me back, seawards,
to a headland of thrift and stone
where July strikes cold with its bluster —
and already there's no getting away,
the native speakers are shouldering my boat
to the slipway. I float her
and fill her with my tackle (raingear,
a sooty kettle), then pay the interpreter
and row out alone into heavy waters,
where the gulls come into their own.

3

So I turn to Clare Island, and approach,
as they line up on the pier
and jostle for place, the forefathers
ready to construe my coming,
unwilling to believe that I am strange
to the old score of grant and annexation.
And I step ashore, deaf to their questions,
my pages blank for the whims of day.
Here I will inscribe readings
for the Clare Island Survey.

4

Gillie or squire in the first photographs,
going far out to give the scale
with a yardstick as a staff,
remote, unnamed, a small notch,
I would be measured against you,
and will lose face, pacing out
in the footsteps of the early workers
to where fatigue compels the heart,
and return then, my face aglow
with a booty of old words, and new echoes.

Manx Shearwater

By day,
on the shore, during this year's holiday
we desired those distant, rocking waters
where shearwaters raft in thousands;

by night,
those islands where they come ashore
as weird calls teeming in the dark.
But, stronger than regret,

one evening,
love rose into us and robbed us of breath.
You knew then those shearwaters
that the storm spends, and wrecks far inland.

Gannet

The gannetry at Grassholm
is a place
we visited together.
We took no photographs;

just memory tells
of the open boat,
our brisk guide
and the brisk sea weather.

Seven miles out was our tryst
where the birds
cover eleven acres
with guano and nests.

And we were all eyes
for the huge, raucous colony
as if those calls were commending
something in ourselves

that found confirmation
in the remote constellation
of Grassholm, Little Skellig, and St Kilda.
After all, we had come to see.

Now the word *gannet*
in our tongue
is sixty-thousand strong
on a whaleback of land surviving

the grey sea and the wind.
There we had nothing to say.
A damp brochure
fluttered at my hand.

Cormorant

The cormorant sat low
on the brimming meniscus of tide
between the bridges,
and vanished

into the river at intervals,
then reappeared, perhaps with an eel
knotted at his bill,
writhing and recalcitrant.

It's no surprise he sometimes
drew a lunchtime crowd:
imagine the coils wrestling with your mouth
as you try to get him inside you,

that this is what sates
those black congregations
drying their wings on weirs
and cold banks, at the ebb.

Grey Heron

It's time to go
when the dark is gathering
over the lagoon,
although you'd still stalk

as far as Rinneanna
after geese and other secrets,
with just a bird book
and a one-track mind.

Why not end the day
as the bat starts,
with home,
and the lure of kind?

When the wind rises
through the reedmace,
and the heron shrieks in the cold,
you know it's time to go.

Golden Eagle

On the coast of Skye
I saw one rise,
spin and diminish,

then found preenings
at a breezy trig point
before the wind snatched them away —

sparks shot from a fire!
Watch them career
into the bygone!

The ledges are cold,
the eyries drenched
in the great desert of Erris

where the last ones
flew into extinction a lifetime ago
above gillies and starvelings.

Kestrel

Took my eye into the air of himself
and threaded it,

sewing me to the sky
with his looped cycle of flight

up the gully,
then traced a noose

around a lowland belfry
and now, in the suburbs,

can needle a spot
above the apex of a gable,

draw the skein
in circles widening out,

and glide back
to the eye of his obsession.

Peregrine

A mewing from the wall of the coum,
then a bold motion —
'none but the best
breed of falcon'.

Higher up, there might be Sinai
shrouded in mist,
but I dawdle
on the rugged steps to heaven

where one bird is master.
No name will call
this barbarian out of the air;
neither *peregrine* nor *seabhac gorm*

will come to my bidding.
My fist's ungloved.
Nothing I can say
will be his jesses or his hood.

Red Grouse

On a windy afternoon
fifteen years ago
we put on flapping jerkins
and set out across a moor

in North Tipperary,
my mother protesting,
my eye greedy
for the promised bird.

So I fly off alone
to a strange hollow over the hill
where the going gets rough
through *fraocháns* and heather,

where I nearly falter
with raindrops weeping
onto my waders —
when I hear it from the outcrop:

the grouse saying *go-back*, *go-back*;
and my father's
following calls
coming into range.

Golden Plover

Darling of water,
little one of rain,
your flocks are slow to settle.
You fly up

in golden ticker-tape,
wheel round, then might
come down again — but no,
you labour upwards, outwards,

still yearning for some
far-off callows dreamed of
in a folklore of flood
that tells of their afterlife,

where those who are blest
alight on the top of a rainbow,
then glide steeply down
to the plashy hollows where it rests.

Lapwing

My first lapwing
was disturbed from the nest.
She called so much
that the whole of Connemara

was appalled.
I was taken away
from the eggs at the centre
of her wild, scolding orbits.

Later, wading through marshland
near La Tène,
the parading birds
rasped down through the air.

And recently, in a stubble field
in Offaly, coming up close,
I caught a *pilibín's* sad eye
glancing at me in reproach.

And I went away again
still thinking of dark blotches
on khaki shells
to be found in the right season.

But don't get dizzy looking up.
Keep your eyes
to the breeding ground
and watch where you step.

Woodcock

The soft wad of the dead bird
was handed to my father.
I remember
brown bands on the crown.

Instead of letting it rest,
I later flushed
two, three, four
from a Scottish birch wood.

Next spring, another one
startled from a bank near Galtee
flew off in a line
that ended in the Ukraine.

And, again,
at dusk in Glengarriff,
there was no mistaking who
was patrolling over the wood.

This is as far
as I have gone,
as close as I have come
to *scolopax rusticola*.

Last year they held
a Geiger counter
to one in Wicklow —
Chernobyl crackled in the box.

Curlew

The greyhound bolted after the hare
over ditch and bank
and up onto the hill
as if the hunt were to end in the air.

I strode across humble country
after her, with curlews
calling through a fine spray of rain
falling on upland fields.

I could stop to wonder how the light,
at the late hour, gathered
in the drops on the rush-flower
that were mild gems of grief,

if the gruff handler's heart
lifts, with the dog he has slipped,
towards the scruffy land.
As I followed into the gorse,

I weighed the curlew with misgivings.
There was the bitch,
her nose in the grass,
sniffing the hare's absence.

Herring Gull

On the foreshore at Tacumshin
I watch what can be seen —
sea-holly, spent cartridges,
a plastic bottle,

then a gull flying off.
The beached whale
is a plump aubergine,
sooty black,

with a vent in its crown,
a spatter of blood,
and a grin sunk
somewhere in the blubber.

Gulls on its head
pecked and tugged,
and blinked
on that gun-runner coast,

where any year now
a castaway will stumble
from the waves
to meet indifferent sand.

Here's a history of distance:
Casement being led off,
Alcock and Brown,
crash-landings,

a Spitfire engine caked with a bluish crust,
then those gulls on a whale
a few minutes ago,
and red when the eye burst.

Guillemot

You'll have seen me pointing to a bird
among gannets on a cliff,
and heard me say *guillemot*,
in the guise of a maker.

I want you to have that name
for the first time,
to say it again
if our love stays unbroken.

If we part,
it will have been a word
between two boats at sea
after their oarsmen have spoken.

Cuckoo

Scarcer now
than when he named himself
to every meadow in the townland
when the hay was down,

as I stood on the butt of the wain,
bedding in what tumbled from the pikes
with *cuck-oo*
repeated from the next acre.

So I drifted off
to stalk nearer the bird.
The song got louder
along the bristly edge of the headland.

I hadn't said a word
when my uncle came
calling 'Seán!'
and so I lost the cuckoo.

Skylark

A shard of mirror on the moor,
an image in the grass,

brought the skylarks
down from heaven

and changed their songs
to little squeaks on glass.

Meadow Pipit

Or *reafóg*, as my father said,
when the small bird on the sward
ran away with its splayed
wing twitching,

not in pain,
but to divert us
from the brood
in the core of a tuft.

And we left,
this much the wiser:
that the little ones
needed us gone.

Now my plane flies in
from where they call them
Wiesenpieper,
and splays both wings to stop.

Away from the airport,
I stalk back
to low pleadings
at the edge of earshot.

Wren

While the valley is filled with rain,
I recall the lip of the wren's nest,
how its fine wattle of brittle stalks
couched and housed my forefinger.

I imagine shelter from deserted fields,
sad clocks and dripping cables.
My streaming windows wait —
until the sun cleaves to glinting hedges

and a child in wellies splashes at the gateway
where the frost once shattered underfoot.
That was Stephen's Day
and the King of the Birds was dead.

Now his song explodes in a briar bush.

Stonechat

Set out with purpose
towards that clump of furze
where a stonechat
is feeding on insects.

You'll flush craneflies
and see them eddy away,
to be caught, too,
for all you know.

When the gorse-bush crackles
as the pods snap open,
watch for the fall of a seed
into the rushes.

Then wait until you see
one pod burst.
The whole bush is blooming
with tiny explosions.

Wheatear

Burren land stripped
to a stone skeleton,
maidenhair in the clint,
the Arctic and Mediterranean

winking at each other
in fine weather,
with wheatears
flitting ahead of the car

as we go down
to *thalassa*, *thalassa*,
dreaming of olives
and vineyards.

Blackbird

after Günter Grass

When Eddie Amsel
was wheeled from the chapel
on the Vistula
after his baptism,

every bird
in the district rose.
The infant was the first
of his famous scarecrows.

Goldcrest

What's in the wood that is not ourselves?

You might well ask of our Sunday walks
through the forestry plantation,
when we defer to what is here
although so much remains unspoken.

We come together to this greying of grass
that might be a fox's path
and might be the spoor that leads
to you, after all these years;

or the scuffs in the bank, the loose tufts
that the badger must have left,
grubbing down to the root
of our silence in this quiet wood.

Show me the lichen I have bruised.
I'll show you the goldcrest.
You can't hear its high pitch anymore,
but when you were young you found its nest.

Chough

With the tower-builders gone from the promontories
I can inspect the fallen stairs,
the chimneys clogged with mortar and twigs,
no gyre there for my late ascendant.

So I go out again and cross
sheep pasture to the edge of the cliff
where the choughs are riding on the updraught.
Their voices are the squeaky hinge

of a door yanked open on old atrocities.
When they settle,
they displace old tenants of the castle,
Macbeth's mad wife, and Yeats,

looking down on small fields inland —
even Malachi Mulligan.
Their bright lobster bills
are a beacon only for themselves.

Hooded Crow

As I climbed that brittle tree
near the tip-head,
the lichen smeared me green.

I wanted the scald crow's egg
fresh and entire,
like those I had seen

in my field-guide,
to blow yolk and white,
and leave a light, rocking shell.

So I rose to the top.
Then I arched an arm
into the lined well

to know what was snug in the nest.
Blind fingers yearned
for a solid clutch.

They came down instead
on hatched life
that was clammy to touch.

Raven

An old crone moving through the wreck
of glamour on a smoking battlefield
teaches this source:

'I had been engrossed.
He tricked me into tricking a hero out,
so I made his crown blood-red,

his locks, henna-brown and yellow —
but then the ne'er-do-well
gave me my reward with his call to war.'

The first mourners venerate his cross
amid the women's weeping
and the bronze raven is cast.

This cold bird will not ascend
and never flap its vans
into Christ's peace.

Her keening holds me down — to the youths
in a circle behind the cathedral
kicking the man on the ground.

Twite

A scant party of finches
is blown across a winter shore
to settle, out of sight.
Follow them, then,

along the wrack of the storm-line.
Let the flowerlets gone to seed
and the trembling grass stalks
that they feed on

be the décor of our days.
These end in a gust across shingle
snatching those twites
back to a darkening coast,

and leave us our subsistence in this:
that as the waves unfold towards night
our mouths will taste
the licking-salts on our sea-brows.

Snow Bunting

Before I could invoke
the snow buntings as snow-flakes

that settle from nowhere,
as fleckings on scree an echo away,

they had parleyed on me.
Relishing their *nivalis*,

I was climbing to conjecture
the merest Eden

when they deserted the stones, lichen, saxifrage
that were to host them.

Yellowhammer

A singing yellowhammer among hooped briars,
between the fuchsia

of a West Kerry hedge, was *siobháinín bhuí*
ag briseadh a croí ag gáirí

while a squall misted in the distance,
then rose in the near leaves

that tossed, and were glazed, and wept.
We stared out past them at chilly acres,

flush with memories of golden birds
and lost domains — until it was all over

and he was the gleaming bunting
that sang to the steaming road.

Coda

Evening on a spit of rock and gravel,
kelp and wrack at the verge, my favourite bay.
After the taut mirror of tide, levels
slacken, then the surge goes racing from me.
The shingle drains, the birds are moving out
over a last concurrence of waters
to feed. Tonight I could be free of them.
My coat flaps and shudders on the wearer,
knocking to know if I am any more
than trail, convergence, go-between.
Creatures that were seen are now flying
out of range, so I must be fledged, in turn,
into convictions that no bird can help
as I take to the empty air, and dare myself.

Notes and Acknowledgements

I am indebted to the Royal Irish Academy's *Biological Survey of Clare Island in the County of Mayo, Ireland*, published in three volumes (Dublin, 1911-15), and to Robert Lloyd Praeger's *The Way that I Went: An Irishman in Ireland* (Dublin, 1937), which led me to it.

The species treated in my survey were originally suggested by the list of Irish names of birds compiled by Seán Mac Giollarnáth in P. G. Kennedy, R. F. Ruttledge and C. F. Scroope, *The Birds of Ireland* (Edinburgh, 1954). I include two species not on that list: Wren and Snow Bunting. The order of species follows the convention established by K. H. Voous in his *List of Recent Holarctic Bird Species* (London, 1977).

Over the years, I have been aided in the field by several guides, but special mention deserves to be made of Roger Tory Peterson, Guy Mountfort, and P. A. D. Hollom's *A Field Guide to the Birds of Britain and Europe*, which has outlived them all. The standard work on the current status of Irish birds is C. D. Hutchinson, *Birds in Ireland* (Carlton, 1989).

I also wish to thank Eithne White and Liam Lysaght for invaluable assistance, and Günter Grass for permission to draw on his novel *Dog Years* ('Blackbird').

Acknowledgements are due to the editors of the following publications, where some of these poems, or earlier versions of them, first appeared: *Cyphers, The Great Book of Ireland, The Honest Ulsterman, The Irish Review, On the Counterscarp, Poetry Ireland Review, Stet, Spirit* (New Jersey).